D0391358

How to Use MailChimp for Beginners:

The Indie Author's Guide to Email Marketing

Adam Netherlund

EnemyOne

Published by **EnemyOne**

St. Catharines, ON

www.enemyone.com

Book & Cover Design by **Adam Geen**

www.adamgeen.com

ISBN-13: 978-1500379209

ISBN-10: 1500379204

How to Use MailChimp for Beginners

Table of Contents

CHAPTER 1:

Introduction

As an indie author it's important to be connected with your fans and have the ability to communicate with them when you have important news to share like a new release or convention appearance.

One of the easiest ways to do that is to have a newsletter and it's important to start one early or you could potentially be limiting yourself as an author.

When you start a newsletter and begin taking email addresses from your fans, you build the foundation that could become very useful to you in the future. Think of it as an inverted pyramid. The small tip is where you are now—just beginning to get those email addresses. As you gain more fans, it starts building, getting just a bit bigger but then over time it gets bigger and bigger like the base of a pyramid.

But how do you get there? Where do you start?

Well, I'm glad you asked.

First things first, who is this book meant for? This book is for beginners who are seeking to use email marketing and specifically MailChimp in their marketing efforts.

There are quite a few different options available to you but I have the most experience using MailChimp so that's where my focus will lie. Some of the alternatives include AWeber, Constant Contact, iContact, Vertical Response, et cetera.

This book is also specifically for people who are not looking to spend a lot of money in order to perform said marketing efforts. It can be expensive trying to get your first book published. I believe everyone should start small at first, an almost grassroots approach until they see some return on investment.

With MailChimp they provide a nice free option where you don't have to pay a monthly fee and it's an attractive option to most indie authors. Until you hit the big time and have a list of more than 2000 subscribers you don't have to pay so don't feel like you have to spend a ton of money to make things proper. If you're looking for something that's not as robust as MailChimp, there's also the option of TinyLetter (http://www.tinyletter.com) which is made by the same company. TinyLetter offers a clean writing experience for people who aren't looking for advanced reporting or bells and whistles in regards to templates. Best of all, it's free up to 3000 subscribers.

In this short book I will show you the ins and outs of setting up your first MailChimp account, walking you through your first campaign and also sharing some tips on building your list. Toward the end of the book I will also be going over some extra features that are entirely up to you whether you want to use them or not.

So let's get started, shall we?

CHAPTER 2:

Taking those First Steps

The first thing you'll need to do is set up an account with MailChimp. You can find their website here. (www.mailchimp.com)

Once you've set up an account, they'll send you an email to confirm the activation. Just click the big blue button to activate your account.

They'll ask you for some personal information. This includes details such as your name, organizational information, your company, your website URL, your address, your industry and your timezone. You'll have the opportunity to upload a Profile Photo if you like at 300px x 300px.

For those of you afraid to list your home address, please be aware that it is part of the FTC's CAN-SPAM law that they are requiring you to do so. But, there are ways around it. One option is to rent a PO Box which can be had in the $60-100/year price range.

For further ideas check out this post from MailChimp. (http://kb.mailchimp.com/article/im-an-artist-and-i-dont-have-a-po-box.-can-i-use-mailchimp)

Items to Note:

• You have the opportunity to import a list of emails into MailChimp (if you have them) at this time under Organization Information.

• The dropdown menu for "Your industry" is used to determine how your campaigns compare to those in your industry. So if you're a restaurant, you would choose "Restaurant and Venue." For the indie author you could choose "Media and Publishing."

• The "Company/Organization" field is mandatory so you can enter your name or possibly the name of your publishing company if you have formed one.

Dashboard

With the finer details out of the way, you'll be presented with your shiny new Dashboard. MailChimp will walk you through a few of the different options helping familiarize yourself with their Dashboard.

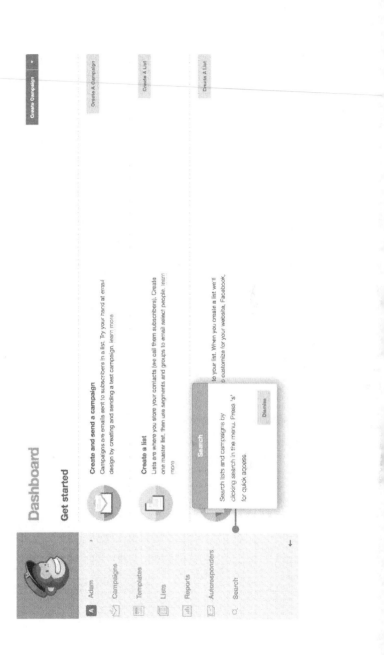

The first thing I'm going to do is head into My Profile. This can be found by clicking the little triangle next to your name (Adam) in this example on the left-hand side of the menu.

There are some security fields I want to fill out just in case someone tries to access my account without my knowledge. You have the option of enabling receiving a message via SMS or Email. I'm going to select Email. You can also register your cell phone for unusual activity through the use of SMS.

Within your account there are also some other menus. These include Billing, Extras, and Rewards. For the purposes of this book, we're operating under the assumption that we will be using a Free Account so I won't worry about that. Let's head into Extras though.

API key

I'm going to get you to set up what's called an API key. This key will come in handy down the road when you want to place a signup form on your website or through a plugin on a WordPress site. Click the button that says "Create a Key" and you're all set. It will automatically show up on a line just above the key button. It's typically this long line of numbers and letters.

So now would probably be a good time to explain what you've just signed up for... I had you sign up for what's called the **Forever Free** plan. Under this plan you can have up to 2000 subscribers to your newsletter. You'll also have the ability to send up to 12, 000 emails. This plan works great for small businesses and individuals. In our example of an indie author it works perfectly as it will take some time to accrue a high amount of subscribers. Although if you're writing in one of the bigger genres like Romance, Erotica or Mysteries you might get there awfully fast! If you find you're about to hit the wall on the amount of subscribers, you can just as easily convert to a Paid account.

Please note: Autoresponders are not available in the Forever Free plan.

Lists

Next we'll be setting up your first List so select that option from the left-hand side of the menu. There's a button on the top-right that says "Create List," click that and away we'll go.

You'll be presented with a couple of options here: List name, Default "from" email, Default "from" name and a box where you can input a reminder of how people got on your list.

Your List name is what you want your newsletter to be called. This could be something like John Doe Newsletter or even a company name.

The Default "from" is kind of self-explanatory but it basically means who do you want it to say that the email is coming from.

The reminder box is there to help serve as a reminder to your subscribers when they get emails from you. This will show up in the footer of the bottom of your emails.

For example, I could write something like:

You are receiving this email because you opted in at my website or through my Facebook Page.

Toward the bottom you also have the option of turning on Summary Notifications. This is useful if you're curious how your list is performing and don't want to sign in to your account all the time.

Signup Forms

You'll have to get people on your list somehow so we'll need to create some signup forms. These can be used on a landing page (a website page that you direct people to), in a widget or call-out area on your webpage, on your Facebook Page or lastly, via a link within a book itself.

To create a signup form you select your List from the left-hand side in the menu. The screen will bring up your list and at the far right next to "Stats" is a little arrow. Click that and select Signup forms from the dropdown menu.

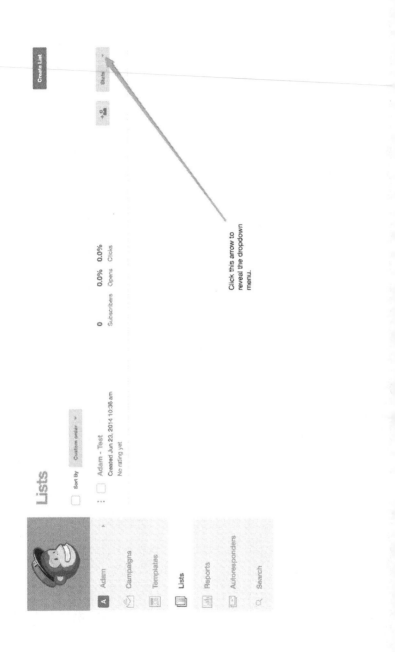

Click this arrow to reveal the dropdown menu.

On the new page you're presented with 5 different options:

- General Forms
- Embedded Forms
- Form Integrations
- Facebook Form
- Tablet Form

Don't worry, you don't have to use all of these options. You can probably get away with just using one or two. When it comes to signup forms, it's a matter of your own personal preference. What kind of information are you looking to get from your subscribers? Would you just like their email? Their first name? Their first and last name? Maybe even some more options like date of birth, zip code/postal code, country? It's entirely up to you. Generally, you don't want to overload your subscribers though as the more information you ask for, the less likely they are to sign up.

Embedded Form

Let's start with the Embedded Form. You'll be using this on a website as it generates the HTML code for you to use. When you select that option you're presented with 4 different options at the top:

- Classic
- Super Slim
- Naked
- Advanced

Classic is the one you'll probably use the most, Super Slim is exactly as it sounds—a slimmed down version, Naked is an "ugly" version with no CSS or JavaScript and Advanced is for well, advanced users who will want to design their own code.

Selecting the Classic version brings up the new page showing your options. A large number of you may even be happy with the way this looks right now and that's perfectly okay. If you're happy with it, click your cursor on the "Copy/Paste" area and copy/paste it onto your website. The Classic version displays field boxes for First Name, Last Name and Email Address. If you find it shows up too big on your website, adjust the "Set form width" area in the Form options fields.

The Super Slim version is great for those users that only want the email address field to be displayed for signup.

Since this book is meant for beginners I won't get into using CSS or JavaScript so that eliminates the Naked and Advanced versions for our purposes.

General Forms

General Forms tends to be what I like to use the most. I find that it provides me with numerous options and the ability to change things up a bit. This is the area where you'd get to experiment with how your signup form looks to your subscribers. One warning ahead of time: there are a lot of options within this area. Don't let it intimidate you!

The first thing I want to point out is at the top, "Forms and response emails." There's another one of those dropdown menus there and within you'll find all the different types of emails you could potentially send to your subscribers. These includes things like:

- Thank you pages
- Confirmation emails
- Unsubscribed confirmation emails
- Surveys
- Forward to a Friend emails

The list is quite extensive. You don't have to set up all of these if you don't want to.

Just below that area is your Signup form URL. **This is extremely important!** I would Copy/Paste this somewhere in your records. It usually begins with something like this: http://eepurl.com/.... (Replace the dots with your unique code.)

Got it recorded somewhere? Good.

There's 3 options in the header: Build it, Design it and Translate it.

Build it

Let's start with Build it. Remember earlier I said you have some leeway on what kind of information you want to get from your subscribers? This is that area. On the right-hand side are some field options that you can add to your signup form. It's as easy as clicking the field option that you want to add and it magically appears on your form. Pretty cool, no?

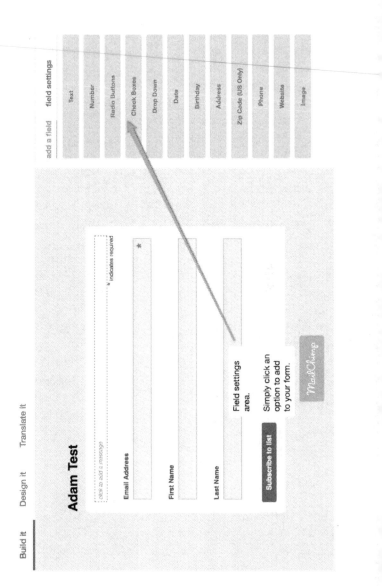

What's that? You added something by accident? No problem. Click the newly added field on your form and at the bottom there will be a plus and minus sign. Click the minus sign to remove it. A new window will pop up asking you to confirm the deletion. Type DELETE in all caps and poof, it's gone. Crisis averted.

You may have also noticed when you clicked the field, some new options appeared on the right-hand side of the page. This is your settings area. You can adjust the label (how it appears), the field tag (the CSS code), whether you want it to be a required field or not, the visibility, and help text. This area will change according to what you're adding or subtracting from the signup form.

At the top of your signup form you have the option of adding a header image and a short message below that if you like. Hover your cursor over these areas and a small window will pop up asking you what you would like to do. If you're adding a header image, the image file manager will show up on your screen and you can edit some of its details. Pay close attention to its width and height, you don't want your header image to be too big or too small. If you find it is a little messed up, just select the image again and punch in different numbers into the boxes. Make sure "Keep proportions" is checked and it will downsize or upsize accordingly.

Design it

In the Design it tab, you're able to adjust some of the colors of the background, text and fields. You also have the ability to adjust the Font Size and Font Family. Run through the various options and adjust as you see fit.

Translate it

You probably won't use this area at all but you also have the option of selecting different languages for your signup form in the Translate it tab.

Form Integrations

I won't get into Form Integrations in terms of the signup form as there's not a lot of info in this area but if you have a WordPress or Squarespace website you might want to have a look as there's links sending you to their respective websites within.

Facebook and Tablet form

The same can also be said about these options. I will talk about Facebook and tablet later in Chapter Five: Extras.

Chapter in Review:

• Fill in all the mandatory fields under your account such as your company, address, organization type, et cetera.

• Add in some additional security options under My Profile so that you will receive SMS or Emails regarding fraudulent uses of your account.

• Create an API key that you will use later on your website or through a plugin on a WordPress website.

• Create your first List!

• Create signup forms

CHAPTER 3:

Building Your Campaign

Whew! Having fun yet? That's quite the previous Chapter, no? Now we're going to start getting into the more complicated sections. (What?! I hear ya.) It's time to build our first Campaign.

Select Campaign from your menu on the left-hand side if you're not there already and then click "Create Campaign." You're presented with a few options. You will typically only use the first one, "Regular ol'Campaign." The third option, "A/B Split Campaign" is useful for when you want to test out different email types, subject lines, or times. (Ie. A newsletter with the subject "Save 20% Today Only" versus "Preferred Customer Sale - Save 20%")

Choose a type of campaign to send:

Regular ol' Campaign
Send a lovely HTML email along with a plain-text alternative version.

Select

Plain-Text Campaign
Send a simple plain-text email with no pictures or formatting.

Select

A/B Split Campaign
Send to two groups to determine the best subject line, from name, or time/day to send campaigns.

Select

RSS-Driven Campaign
Send content from an RSS feed to a list.

Select

Email Beamer

Did you know you can send campaigns directly from your favorite email client?

Learn more

Campaigns can be boiled down to 5 basic steps which you'll find at the bottom of your screen: Recipients (Your List), Set Up (Entering details about your campaign and tracking), Template (Selecting a template), Design (Writing your newsletter), and Confirm.

Recipients: Select List

If you have more than one list, you would select which one you want to send the campaign to but most of the time it'll just be pre-selected for you.

Set Up: Campaign Info

After clicking the Create Campaign button, you are presented with a new screen where you will start filling in some details. First, name your campaign (this is for your records only, the customer will not see this), enter your subject line and the From fields should be filled out already because it is grabbing the info from your profile. You have the option of personalizing the "To" field as well so you can either tick it on or off.

Campaign Info

Name your campaign

Internal use only. Ex: "Newsletter Test#4"

Email subject

150 characters remaining

How do I write a good subject line?

From name

100 characters remaining

Use something subscribers will instantly recognize, like your company name.

From email address

☐ **Manage replies from my subscribers** Paid accounts only

When enabled, we'll generate a special reply-to address for your campaign. We'll filter "out of office" replies, then thread conversations into your subscribers' profiles and display them in reports.

☑ **Personalize the "To:" field**

Include the recipient's name in the message using merge tags to make it more personal and help avoid spam filters. For example, *|FNAME|* *|LNAME|* will show "To: Bob Smith" in the email instead of "To: bob@example.com". This is more personal and may help avoid spam filters.

Specify *|MERGETAGS|* for recipient name

|FNAME|

Set Up: Tracking and Social Media

The next area is for your tracking purposes. This will help you get some analytical information on your subscribers. You can track the "opens" and "clicks" of your subscribers. (We'll be delving into analytics in the next Chapter.)

There are also a number of other options available to you but they require you opening other accounts or adding information on your website.

If you will be selling products or services on your website you may want to consider using the options: Google Analytics link tracking and Ecommerce360 link tracking.

At the bottom you have the ability to connect both your Twitter and Facebook accounts. Once they're connected and you send out a newsletter, it will auto-post to these accounts with a link to your newsletter. Think of it as an extra way to increase your reach on social media. It's entirely up to you if you want to connect them or not.

Tracking

☑ **Track opens**
Discover who opens your campaigns by tracking the number of times an invisible web beacon embedded in the campaign is downloaded. Learn more

☑ **Track clicks** Required on free accounts
Discover which campaign links were clicked, how many times they were clicked, and who did the clicking.

☑ **Track plain-text clicks** Required on free accounts
Track opens and clicks in the plain-text version of your email by replacing all links with tracking URLs. Learn more

☐ **Google Analytics link tracking**
Track clicks from your campaigns all the way to purchases on your website.
Requires Google Analytics on your website.

☐ **Ecommerce360 link tracking**
Track visitors to your website from your MailChimp campaigns, capture order information, and pass that information back to MailChimp. Then you can view purchase details, conversions, and total sales on the reports page. You can also set up segments based on your subscribers' purchase activity. Learn more

☐ **ClickTale link tracking**
Gain insight to how subscribers interact with your email content.
Requires ClickTale on your website.

☐ **Goal tracking** Paid accounts only
Track where subscribers go on your site, then trigger autoresponders or segment your list based on what pages they've visited.

☐ **Track stats in Salesforce or Highrise**
First, enable Salesforce or Highrise in Account > Integrations.

Social Media

☐ Auto-tweet after sending

Connect To Twitter

☐ Auto-post to Facebook after sending

Connect To Facebook

Templates and Themes

Next we'll be choosing a Template to use for our campaign. There are a TON of options so I can't really tell you what to do here. Some people prefer very basic templates whereas others are happy with something a little more artistic. The choice is yours! I find I tend to lean toward the "Right Sidebar" option.

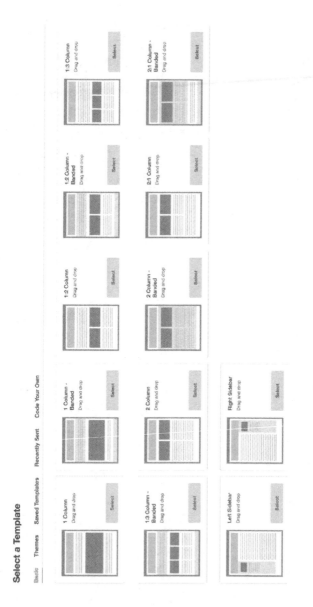

If you click Themes, a new page will come up with some pre-made options for you grouped by categories. They include things like: Art, Non-Profits, Newsletters, eCommerce, Birthday, Real Estate, Fitness, Holiday, Photography, Restaurant, et cetera. Browse around and see if anything catches your fancy.

Design: Designing and Writing Your Email

Now it's time for the hard stuff. Luckily for you MailChimp has made this quite a bit easier than in the past. On the right-hand side of the page will be options that you can drag and drop into your email. These could include items such as: buttons, dividers, boxes, image boxes, social buttons, captions, et cetera.

On the left-hand side is the preview of your email while it's in progress. It will auto-update as you make changes and type.

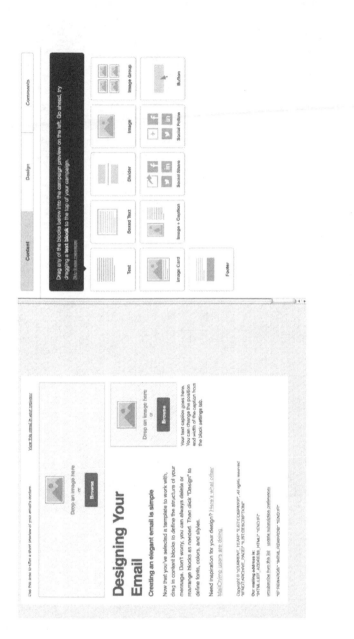

Most templates come with the basic necessities like a header, short preview area, footer, body and possibly some sidebars. You mouse over these "blocks" to select the different sections. It will pop up with a dark gray border around the section with some options. These include: drag to reorder, edit block, duplicate block, delete block.

Keep an eye on the right-hand side as you select these "blocks." New windows will open up and that will be where you will be entering your information whether it's text, links, file names, etc.

Also, keep in mind you can play with headings, bolding and colors as well.

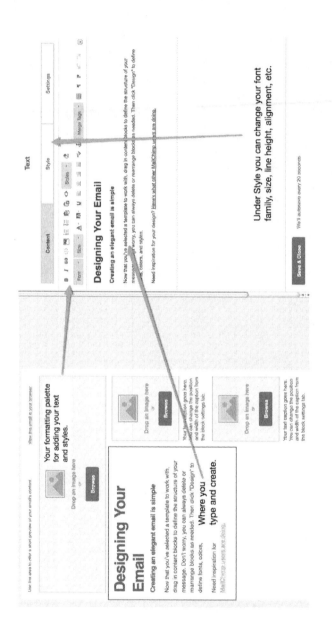

Your formatting palette for adding your text and styles.

Where you type and create.

Under Style you can change your font family, size, line height, alignment, etc.

Confirm: Final Check

Once you've completed the final design, you're pretty much finished so now's the time to verify that everything is set up correctly. You have the option to edit areas if you like and MailChimp will help remind you of things you may have forgotten.

And that's really all there is to it. The hard work is over.

Bonus Tip!

You'll want to enter into Preview Mode or send a Test Email to verify the contents of your email and to make sure everything turned out okay. Take the time to go over your spelling and grammar but also to verify that your images and links are working correctly. You want that first impression to be a great one. You can head into the Preview Mode by clicking at the top-right in the menu.

If you're okay with everything after that then it's time to schedule the campaign. You can set the date and time under the free plan, the paid feature allows you to do some extra options.

Chapter in Review:

• Choose the type of Campaign you want to send out to your subscribers.

• Select List (Usually by default but if you have more than one, make sure you're sending to the right one.)

• Name your Campaign and its appropriate information.

• Select a Template or Theme.

• Design and write your Campaign including images and links.

- Verify, confirm and schedule your Campaign.
- Don't forget to send a test email or preview it just in case to make sure your links are working correctly and everything looks A-okay.

CHAPTER 4:

Understanding Analytics

So let's say it's now a month later or so and you've been sending out your Campaigns and you're trying to make sense of all these numbers. What do they mean?!

Well, don't fret. I'm here to teach you a thing or two about some of those numbers. In this Chapter I'll help you understand a little something called analytics. Once you get going and start getting some numerical feedback on your campaigns and subscribers you'll see something like this when you log into your account. You'll have to forgive me but I've blacked out some of my personal information in the graphic but I think you'll get the gist of it.

On the dashboard there's a couple of things it's telling me right away:

- The percentages of my last Campaign at the top under "Recent Campaigns."
- The average List Growth for the past couple of months (the graphic is cut off slightly at the bottom.)
- The percentages of my Top 5 campaigns that have gone out.

Open Rates

Opens or Open Rate is a measure of how many people on your list open (or view) a particular campaign. The open rate is normally expressed as a percentage, and is calculated as follows: So a 20% open rate would mean that of every 10 campaigns delivered to an inbox, 2 were actually opened.

Now, you'll find opinions vary wildly on what a true open rate percentage is, especially with the addition of Gmail's new tabbed inbox. You can find out more about how that's affecting your open rates here via MailChimp's blog. (http://blog.mailchimp.com/how-gmail-tabs-affect-your-email-marketing-an-update)

Open rates are typically tracked using a transparent 1x1 pixel, or small transparent tracking image, that is embedded in outgoing emails. When the browser used to display the email requests that image, then an "open" is recorded for that email by the image's host server. The email will not be counted as an open until one of the following occurs:

- The subscriber enables the images in the email or

• The subscriber interacts with the email by clicking on a link

In addition, many email clients block images by default, or the recipient may elect to receive text-only versions of an email. In both cases, no image call can ever be made, further reducing the accuracy of your open rate percentages. There's also the distinct possibility that your campaign might have hit their Spam folder or Junk Mail.

Keep in mind that your open rate will vary according to your industry. Experiment, try different things, and look at segmenting your list to try and make a change to your open rate. You can find a post from MailChimp on email benchmarks here on their website. (http://mailchimp.com/resources/research/email-marketing-benchmarks)

To save you from having to check, this is what they list our industry as:

Media and Publishing—22.93%(Open Rate), 5.14% (Click Rate)

Clicks

Your Click or click-through rate percentage is the number of subscribers who click one or more links in your campaign and land on your website, blog, or wherever else you're asking them to go. More simply, click-through rates represent the number of clicks that your campaign generated. Click-through rate, is expressed as a percentage, and calculated by dividing the number of click-throughs by the number of tracked messages opened.

You would use these numbers to understand the

effectiveness and success of your campaign. In general there is no ideal click-through rate although I prefer to see a higher number. The higher the number, the more interaction and engagement I'm getting from them after all.

It can vary based on the type of campaign sent, how frequently your campaigns are sent, how the list of subscribers is segmented, how relevant the content of the campaign is to your list, and many other factors. Even time of day can affect click-through rate. For example, studies show Sunday appears to generate considerably higher click-through rates on average when compared to the rest of the week.

For you, as an indie author, click-through rate would be extremely important and valuable as you would be including a link to your newly released title on Amazon or some other retailer.

Reports

If you dive into the Reports menu on the left-hand side of your general main menu, you'll find some details pertaining to all of your campaigns.

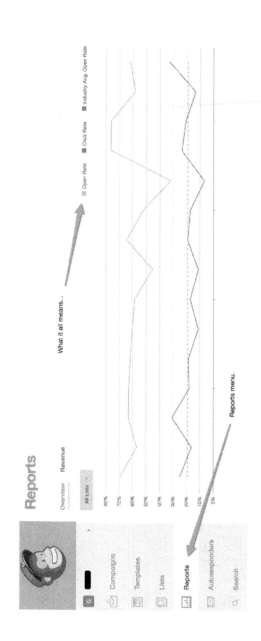

If you scroll down further you'll see a list of all of your campaigns at a quick glance. You also have the option of viewing a report of each one. I'll show you an example of that in a second.

I like to browse through here every so often to get a feel for how my campaigns are performing and to get an idea of which ones my subscribers seem to enjoy.

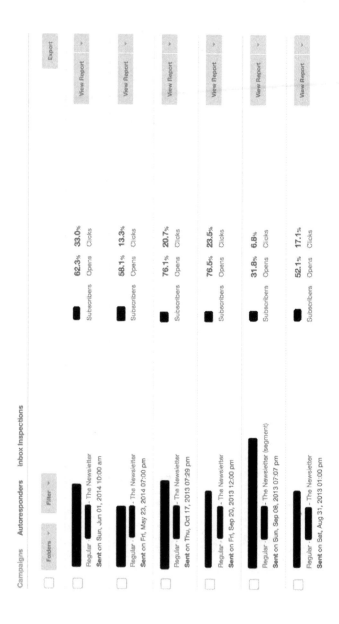

Let's look at one of those campaigns in depth. This is probably the busiest looking page within your account but don't let it overwhelm you! You can do it. In this example, I'm going to look at my most recent campaign —the one at the top of the list in the graphic. This is what it looks like:

Reports

Overview   Activity ▾   Links   Social   E-commerce   Conversations   Advanced

Delivered Sun, Jun 01, 2014 10:00 am

View Email · Download · Print · Share

Recipients

List		
Subject		

Open rate 62.3%

List avg	58.3%
Industry avg (Other)	19.2%

Click rate 33.0%

List avg	18.0%
Industry avg (Other)	3.1%

Opened	35 Clicked	0 Bounced	1 Unsubscribed

Successful deliveries	53.0%
Total opens	81
Last opened	6/3/14 11:03AM
Forwarded	1

Clicks per unique opens	100.0%
Total clicks	
Last clicked	8/22/14 12:15AM
Abuse reports	0

If I were to scroll down I'd also be given a ton of other information but for the purposes of this book I'd have to black out all kinds of personal information so you'll have to accept my apologies. I can summarize what you'll find though! It includes:

- 24-hour performance in a flow chart of your Opens and Clicks.
- Top links clicked with the exact link and the count of clicks.
- Subscribers with most opens including the count of opens and their email addresses.
- Social performance
- Top locations by opens with percentages by countries and map graphic on the right-hand side.

For the most part I think the graphic I've included makes things pretty self-explanatory. Within the report you're able to look at how your campaign performed and what seemed to get the most engagement out of your subscribers.

Are they clicking and going off to where you wanted them to go? If not, why?

Over time you'll find this feature very useful because you're not going to remember everything you did in the past. So if I find one campaign in particular didn't perform up to snuff I can go back and see how similar ones compared in the past. The original email you sent out is accessible from here as well if you can't recall what it looked like—just click "View Email." It's at the top under the Delivery date.

Some of you may have noticed that at the very top

under **Reports,** there's some other headings as well. (Overview, Activity, Links, et cetera.) In there you'll find even more goodies.

By clicking "Activity" you're presented with things like: Didn't Open, Sent to, Clicked, Bounced, Unsubscribed, et cetera. If you head into these areas you'll have their email address, name (if provided), Member Ratings, and Last Changed Dates.

The **Links** heading will provide you with a complete listing of all the links you used in your campaign and percentages on Total Clicks and Unique Clicks. You'll also see a "Click Map" which I like a lot. Once clicked your original email shows up with little bars and percentages over the areas that your subscribers clicked. I'm a visual person so it helps to visualize where they're clicking and possibly reading. I've learned a couple of interesting things this way… for example, I didn't think people would click my header image or even some of the information in the footer but they appear to do so.

The next 4 groupings (Social, E-commerce, Conversations, and Advanced) will not work unless you enable them or set up a paid account.

Chapter in Review:
- Understanding analytics
- Open Rates and Clicks
- Reports (How are your campaigns performing?)
- Using the sub-menus of Overview, Activity, and Links.

CHAPTER 5:

Ideas for Building that Mailing List

One of the most important things for you to be doing when it comes to email marketing is, wait for it, getting people on your list! Imagine that, right? They say the money is in the list.

As an indie author I strongly believe it is one of the most important things that an author should both have AND be working on at all times. Their list of priorities could really be simplified down to two things: Writing books to sell and a list of people to sell those books to.

The great thing about having an email list is that it's yours to keep forever. Yes, people move on... they unsubscribe, they change emails, they stop responding to your emails, et cetera but it's still yours... One day you could have over 10, 000 people on your list or even 50, 000. The sky's the limit and it's a perfect way for you to communicate directly with your fan base. It's not Facebook, Twitter, or Amazon where they're owned by someone else and could potentially harm your business if they make changes. (I'm sure most of you would agree that Facebook's recent changes have drastically altered how effective it's become to brand building.)

But what if you're stuck for ideas? Well, let me try and help. Here are some ideas that you could try to build that list up if you feel like you're struggling.

• Create a lead-gen offer—like a free ebook/short story—and require visitors to provide their email address in order to download it. Another idea could be bonus content such as alternate scenes, scenes from the cutting room floor, alternate POVs or cool background materials like artwork, maps, etc.

• Create a Twitter ad campaign offering a lead-gen offer just like above.

• Promote an online contest or run a giveaway, and have people sign up with their email address to gain entry. (Rafflecopter, Free Kindle Giveaway, etc.)

• Put a signup link virtually everything you can think of! This includes:

-In the front/back of your ebook/paperback

-On your website (Make sure it's front and center above the fold.)

-On your author pages at retailers or product pages

-In your email signature

-On your Facebook Page via an app or thru MailChimp

• If at a trade show/convention, you could use an

iPad and use one of MailChimp's mobile apps. (Check out the next Chapter for more on this.)

- If you've got some chops and maybe are a non-fiction author, host a webinar and collect the emails during registration.

- Add a QR code to your print marketing that people can scan. This could be your paperbacks, bookmarks, posters, handouts, or other marketing materials.

- Encourage your current subscribers to share your campaigns. Utilize the "Forward to a Friend" option within your emails.

- Utilize Google AdWords and create an ad which when clicked takes them to a signup landing page on your website.

- Guest posting is a great way to get in front of a larger audience. Make good use of your About the Author bio box. Use a sentence to encourage readers to sign up for your awesome list or describe your incentive. Include a link to a landing page on your website.

- On your Facebook Page/Twitter let people know that you've been sending exclusive offers to your list. It may prompt them to want to sign up because they realize they're missing out on all the fun. (Cover reveals, exclusive short stories, book previews, beta reads, ARC giveaways, etc.)

- Create a subscribe via comment box on your website. If your visitor is already entering their email address somewhere like in a comment box, it only makes sense that adding a check mark to also subscribe to your newsletter would increase conversions. There are plugins (http://wordpress.org/plugins/mailchimp-for-wp) for this sort of thing.

- Similarly, if you have products or services for sale directly on your site consider adding a "Check here to subscribe to my super-awesome-sauce weekly newsletter" tick box to your process.

- Received an email from a fan? Consider asking them if they've signed up and if not, ask if you can add them. (I realize this isn't for everyone but some people have had success with it.)

Chapter in Review:
- Get people on your List!

CHAPTER 6:

Extras

This Chapter is all about odds and ends. They're subjects that I could have fit in elsewhere but I didn't want you to get too distracted by some shiny new thing so I opted to keep them toward the end of the book.

We'll be looking at mobile, WordPress plugins, additional signup forms, segments/groups, and a few additional small things.

But first, let's talk about sending out those updates.

Sending out Those Updates

How often you send out is entirely up to you! You don't want to pester them weekly or anything like that. Monthly is pretty good especially if you're a fast writer and can keep up with the demand. At the bare minimum you probably want to email your subscribers once every

2 months. If you find you can't write books fast enough to warrant an email every 2 months then start thinking about things you could update them on.

The idea here is that you want your subscribers to get used to seeing you in their inbox. You don't want them to forget about you and unsubscribe because they don't remember why they signed up in the first place! I've seen some authors update their readers on what they're reading, suggesting other author's books in their genre, and even sharing some personal stuff like signings, vacations, etc. Choose a schedule and try to stick to it. If it's been awhile and you've gone off track, try to remedy the situation immediately.

Tips on Writing Your Campaigns

• Try to remember to give your campaign a purpose —a single point. Think about what action you're trying to get them to take. This will make your life easier and give your campaign focus. Is it to purchase a book, leave a review, read/comment on a blog post, answer a survey? Put your call-to-action in at least 2 different spots. Repeat yourself since people love to skim read. Spell out your links to get them to take action. Don't just write "click here." Tell them what you want them to do and use all of the words for the link.

Example link message: *Click here to download an exclusive short story and share this email!*

• Use the post script to add your second call-to-action. These funny asides are actually the second most read part of your message.

• Write the body of your campaign as if you're writing to a person. Give it that personal, friendly touch as if you were writing to someone you know. Write like you speak and don't be afraid to show people you're excited.

• Use short paragraphs and break up that text! You don't want readers to face a wall of endless text. Keep an eye on your flow to make sure their eyes move naturally down the page. Remember, people have busy lives and we're constantly on the move. Make it easier for them. If you find you want to ramble consider writing a snippet and then add a link that says "Read More" and send them to a blog post on your website where you can continue your train of thought. (Ie. Your most recent trip to a book conference.)

• Read your email out loud the same way you would for your own writing!

MailChimp Mobile

I found out about MailChimp mobile (http:// mailchimp.com/features/mailchimp-mobile) a little late in the game but man, it is so much fun! MailChimp mobile is an app available on Android 4.0+ and iOS 7.0+. With this app you have access to everything in your account right in the palm of your hand. So if you're on the move somewhere and are curious about how you're most recent campaign is performing just open it up and look.

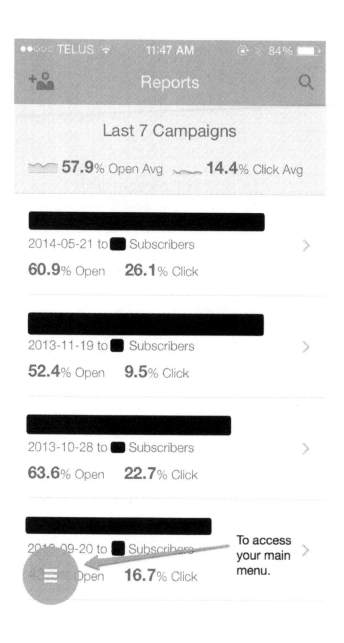

FYI, if you have more than one account with MailChimp, you can easily toggle between all the different accounts.

They also update the app quite a bit so you're constantly getting new features and they love to make adjustments so all of the information you need is front and center.

So yeah, get it and use it. A huge time-saver.

SMS for Events (Gather)

Gather (https://gather.mailchimpapp.com) is another app available on Android 4.0+ and iOS 6.0+. Gather lets you text message your MailChimp subscribers to keep them updated during events. So if you're at an event or maybe even running an event, you could send them alerts on parking snafus, long line-ups, table number changes, etc. But the best part is they can reply back to you as if it was a text message. You start by creating a web form with your phone number then invite attendees to sign up for text alerts during the event. (They can also choose to be added to your list if they're not already on it.) Once the event is over, all data disappears. No privacy issues to worry about!

Chimpadeedoo Tablet form

Chimpadeedoo (http://mailchimp.com/features/mobile-signup-forms) is a mobile signup form for your iPad or Android tablet. It runs on Android 4.0+ and iOS 5.0+. It collects the email addresses and stores them locally on the tablet even when you're not online. Once you connect, it pushes the email addresses into your MailChimp account.

You can add your own logo and background or use

one of their custom themes. You can customize fonts, colors, buttons, images and more. Great idea for a trade show or convention!

WordPress Plugins

MailChimp List Subscribe Form (http:// wordpress.org/plugins/mailchimp) is great for adding a simple signup form on your website. You can add it as a widget in a sidebar or use shortcodes in the body of a post. It features some basic customization options but would require more advanced knowledge of CSS to spruce it up.

MailChimp for Wordpress (http://wordpress.org/ plugins/mailchimp-for-wp) is another plugin for adding a signup form on your website. This is the one I'm using currently and there's also a paid version if you want some more robust features and abilities.

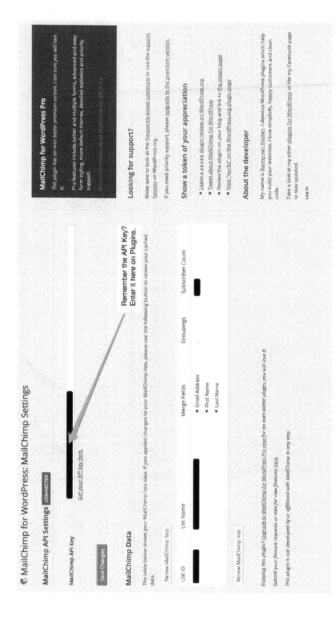

And if you'll recall waaay back at the beginning of this book I had you set up an API Key, the above is an example of why I had you do that. Most plugins will use either your API Key or List ID so it doesn't hurt to set it up.

Easy MailChimp Forms (https://wordpress.org/plugins/yikes-inc-easy-mailchimp-extender) is another plugin for signup forms. I've used this one before as well and I believe it's still active on one of my other websites. You can add forms to posts, pages or sidebars with shortcodes, widgets or template tags. Again, an API Key is required.

MailChimp Form by ContactUs (http://wordpress.org/plugins/mailchimp-form) The MailChimp Form by ContactUs.com integrates the ContactUs.com lead acquisition tools and cloud-based lead management platform to your MailChimp account. The form captures the lead and sends it to specific MailChimp lists automatically. You can set it to no op-in, opt-in, double opt-in and also add CAPTCHA to avoid spam. It requires a ContactUs.com account.

In the end, there are a TON of MailChimp related plugins that you could try out and download for yourself. I can't cover all of them as there's way too many to list.

Segmentations

Sometimes you may only want to email key subscribers, that's when segmentation comes into play. In your account you'll notice subscribers have a "Member Rating" with some stars beside their email address. To come up with a member rating, MailChimp tracks open and click data and measures that against your sending frequency.

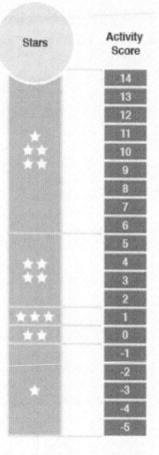

The five star system is based on a twenty point activity score, and they weigh those activity scores unevenly. So the higher the star, the more engaged your subscriber is with your content.

In order for member ratings to accurately measure engagement, subscribers have to lose points for not engaging with your email. They handle that by decrementing activity scores after you send your campaign. Don't panic! They don't decrement these scores every time you send an email. Instead, they factor in your send frequency.

Send Frequency	Decrement Frequency
Once a month or less	Every 2 emails
Up to once a week	Every 3 emails
Up to twice a week	Every 4 emails
More than twice a week	Every 5 emails

But back to segments... what if you have some people who have never opened any of your emails? Should they stay on your list? Hard to say for sure, but I've scrubbed my list before because I'd rather have engaged people on my list.

To do this we would create a Segment. Head to your list and click the name of your list to view your subscribers. Under "View subscribers" is "Segments" and "Subscribed," we want to click Segments and in the dropdown menu—New Segment.

In the first menu select "Member Rating." In the second menu select "is less than," and lastly, select 2 stars. Click the "Preview Segment" button.

Please keep in mind they may have only just joined

your list so you don't want to do too much just yet. If you click "Date Added" in the far right column it will sort the dates for you. You'd be looking for email addresses associated with older dates in order to make sure you're unsubscribing the right people.

If you know who you want to unsubscribe from your list it's as easy as selecting the boxes next to their email addresses and hitting Unsubscribe from the Action box that pops up.

Even if you didn't want to delete people from your list, learning about Segments is a good thing to know as you could do the complete opposite and send an email to your most engaged fans. Just perform the same action but change it to 5 stars and at the right-hand side select "Send to Segment."

You can also save Segments. Simply assign the conditions, save the segment, and it'll update anytime you're ready to send.

Facebook Page Signup Form

If you head into your Account Settings then click Integrations, you can connect your Facebook account to add a signup form to your FB Page. Log into FB, select your list and it will authorize the connection.

If you're using a main Facebook account but manage several Pages underneath that main name (like a pen name for example), that's okay. It will use your main name and then you select which Page you want it to go on. There's only a couple of things that you can customize doing it this way but it does the trick in my opinion.

CHAPTER 7:

Resources

Throughout this book I have included numerous hyperlinks to various websites on the internet so I thought it might be useful to reference them again here in the Resources area. I've separated it out by Chapter to make it a bit easier to find what you might be looking for.

Chapter 2: Taking those First Steps
MailChimp website - www.mailchimp.com
I don't have a PO Box - http://kb.mailchimp.com/article/im-an-artist-and-i-dont-have-a-po-box.-can-i-use-mailchimp

Chapter 4: Understanding Analytics
Gmail affecting Open Rates - http://blog.mailchimp.com/how-gmail-tabs-affect-your-email-

marketing-an-update

Email benchmarks - http://mailchimp.com/ resources/research/email-marketing-benchmarks

Chapter 5: Ideas for Building that Mailing List

MailChimp WordPress plugin - http://wordpress.org/ plugins/mailchimp-for-wp

Chapter 6: Extras

MailChimp Mobile App - http://mailchimp.com/ features/mailchimp-mobile

SMS for Events (Gather) - https:// gather.mailchimpapp.com

Chimpadeedoo Tablet Form - http:// mailchimp.com/features/ mobile-signup-forms

MailChimp List Subscribe Form (WordPress plugin) - http:// wordpress.org/plugins/mailchimp

MailChimp WordPress plugins - http:// wordpress.org/plugins/mailchimp-for-wp

Easy MailChimp Forms (WordPress plugin) - https:// wordpress.org/ plugins/yikes-inc-easy-mailchimp-extender

MailChimp Form by ContactUs (WordPress plugin) - http:// wordpress.org/plugins/mailchimp-form

CHAPTER 8:

Closing Remarks

Well, we've reached the end of our journey. I hope you've learned a thing or two about MailChimp, email marketing, and the power of sending campaigns to inboxes. Before I go I want to thank you for reading this book and I welcome your comments, feedback, or even emails on how you made out with your newly acquired skill-set.

If you could be so kind to leave me an honest review wherever you purchased this book that would be greatly appreciated!

If you'd like to get in touch with me I can be reached via the following channels:

www.adamnetherlund.com
www.facebook.com/adamnetherlund

www.twitter.com/adamnetherlund

Sign up for my newsletter and get first notification of new releases, exclusive previews, and subscriber-only freebies! No spam, and I'll never share your email with anyone. (I hate spam, too.)

I'm currently working on my first fiction novel in the crime/thriller genre so expect some fiction related emails as well.

You can sign up here: bit.ly/adamnetherlund

Thank you very much and let's get cracking on those emails!

About the Author

Adam Netherlund has worked in two bookstores in his young life and it was there that his passion for books began to really take hold. Adam enjoys reading mysteries, thrillers, and pulp books from days long past. He is currently working on his first crime thriller entitled *Eyes of the Dead,* the first in a series, which is expected to be released in Fall 2014. He lives in Ontario, Canada with his wife and their pug, Vincent.

Made in the USA
San Bernardino, CA
25 July 2016